For Travis, Austin, Carson, Mom, Dad, and Kurby.
You all make my life sweeter, and I love you.

Praise for
Sweet Treats for the Holidays

"Norene Cox is a genius at turning ordinary, store-bought items into the most adorable sweet treats! I'm continually blown away by her creativity!"

– Jenny Keller, baker, author, and founder of *jennycookies.com*

"Norene Cox is one of our most popular contributors on *New Day Northwest* because of her endless creativity and whimsical style! Everything she does is infused with fun, color, and an eye for delightful detail. Norene is also a mom's mom, creating projects that can easily include the whole family and make any celebration special. She's a gem!"

– Margaret Larson, host of *New Day Northwest* television show

"If you are what you eat, this book is an invitation to be adorable and sweet… and brimming with pure holiday joy. "

– Jessie Oleson, author, illustrator, and creator of *cakespy.com*

"This book is a must-have for the holiday hostess—filled to the brim with the most creative and unique holiday treats anyone could imagine! Norene will astound you with her array of adorable edible creations, and will show you how to wow your guests this season!"

– Mindy Cone, cookbook author and founder of *getcreativejuice.com*

INTRODUCTION

For ten consecutive years, I served as a room mother for my boys when they were in elementary school and I loved every minute of it. However, it was the school district's policy that homemade food was not allowed at any classroom parties for food allergy reasons. I purchased snack cakes and candies from the grocery store and I showed all the kids how to really play with their food! It was crafting and sweet treats all rolled into one, and it was oh so much fun!

When people told me to enjoy my kids when they were little because time flies, they sure weren't kidding. Hot Wheels were soon traded in for real wheels, and spelling bees were replaced with SAT's. My boys are now in high school and college. How I miss those holiday classroom parties! In fact, one day I was driving home and noticed a bunch of cars parked alongside the road next to my boys' old grade school. It dawned on me that it was Valentine's Day! Tears actually welled up in my eyes, since I really didn't realize it was Valentine's Day until that moment.

Seeing how sad I was, my husband suggested that I start blogging about my "room mom treats." He said I still had so many good ideas that I should share. So I immediately put together my website to see if anyone out there liked cute food ideas for the holidays. I wanted to make sure my treats stayed "kid friendly" and easy to create.

I wasn't certain if using store-bought cakes and cookies actually constituted a recipe, but to my delight, I had a tremendous response from people all over the world (and even Martha Stewart herself)! It was so refreshing to know that there were people like me who wanted to make homemade treats, but didn't want to start from scratch. Busy moms, especially ones with small children, wanted to get right to decorating treats with their kids without having to wait for cakes to bake or cookies to cool.

It's more fun to get busy creating with lots of bright candy, cookies, and store-bought treats. Familiar ingredients that can spark the imagination in any kid, or the kid inside you! I like to call what I do "edible crafting with a heavy dose of cuteness." Because let's face it—it's one thing to make a tasty treat, and quite another to make it so cute that people smile and say, "Awwwww!"

I'm not a professional baker, and my pastry decorating training comes from watching random videos on YouTube. Anyone can make these sweet treats by following my recipes! I took my love of being a room mom, writing, photography, and sweets, and wrapped it all up into my cute candy-coated blog. The amazing response to my website and constant requests for more has finally resulted in this book that I have happily poured my heart into.

Tips and Tricks

HAVE FUN!

The main ingredient for making cute food is FUN! Your imagination is the best tool for creating adorable desserts. Feel free to make substitutions for candy and such. Use M&M's instead of jelly beans, Life Savers in place of mints, brownies rather than Rice Krispies Treats, or homemade instead of store-bought cookies. Don't be afraid to put your own personal spin on these sweet treats.

GET STARTED!

Here are a few basic tips and tricks for making your candy creations even cuter.

DIP IT!

Candy Coating

The two main types of candy coating I like to use are the bags of wafer candy melts and the bark-type candy coatings like Candiquik.

Candy coating cookies using either wafers or bark is easy if you follow these simple steps:

GET ORGANIZED!

Before starting, make sure you have all your ingredients and tools handy. If any kids are helping, have small, personal portions of candy and sprinkles for each child.

1. Melt your candy coating in a microwave according to the package instructions. Pour the coating in a deep container and dip the cookie in the melted coating until completely submerged. Lift it out with a fork and tap it against the container to remove any excess coating.

2. Carefully slide the coated cookie onto parchment paper to set.

FLIP IT!

A great tip for decorating store-bought sugar cookies is to flip them over and create your masterpiece on the flat underside.

DECORATE IT!

A can of ready-to-spread frosting, cookie icing, or food coloring mist can brighten up a cookie, cupcake, or any treat!

EMBELLISH IT!

Sprinkles

I admit that I have somewhat of a sprinkle obsession. I collect sprinkles in all shapes and sizes, all colors and textures, and for all holidays and occasions. Racks and stacks of them. But here is a rundown of the most common sprinkles you will be using in this book.

Sugar Sprinkles

Also known as sanding sugar, these sprinkles are probably the most common and resemble fine sugar. They come in all colors of the rainbow.

Confetti

Flat, round discs in pastel or primary colors.

Jumbo Shapes

Extra large flat sprinkles with circle, tree, heart, and snowflake shapes, to name a few.

Small Shapes

These sprinkles are sometimes called quins and come in all different shapes and holiday themes.

Pearls

Small round balls of sugar, but be careful—these can be hard on your teeth!

Nonpareil

Super tiny balls that like to bounce all over your kitchen counter.

Sugar Crystals

Sugar sprinkles that have a large grain and course texture.

Dragées

Small round balls of sugar coated with a metallic finish.

Candy

Crafting with candy is the best part of making cute food. There are so many bright colors, shapes and sizes, and yummy flavors and textures that you can let your imagination run wild! Grocery stores, gas stations, and convenience or party stores all have an assortment of candies that will spark your creativity. I love to go to grocery stores that sell candy in bulk bins so I can pick and choose how many I want and the colors I need.

Cookies

Transform store-bought cookies into super cute treats. Look at them as a blank canvas to embellish upon, and turn ordinary cookies into extraordinary ones!

More Sweet Stuff

Graham crackers, Rice Krispies Treat bars, marshmallows, cupcakes, and mini donuts are just a few store-bought supplies that can make life easier. Keep these staples on hand so you can make edible crafts at a moment's notice.

FIND IT!
Resources and Suppliers

If you have difficulty finding items listed in the recipes at your local grocery or craft stores, here are some online resources and suppliers:

Edible Markers

Americolor: www.americolorcorp.com

Candy Coating

CandiQuik: www.candiquik.com

Make 'n Mold: www.makenmold.com

Wilton: www.wilton.com

Specialty and Seasonal Candy

Candy.com: www.candy.com

Candy Warehouse: www.candywarehouse.com

Candy Eyes

Wilton: www.wilton.com

Sixlets Candies

SweetWorks: www.sweetworks. net

Chocolate Truffles

Lindt: www.lindtusa.com

Jet-Puffed Marshmallows

Kraft: www.kraftrecipes.com/products/jet-puffed

Chocolate Gelt

Chocolate Gelt: www.chocolategelt.com

Food Coloring Mist

Wilton: www.wilton.com

Sprinkles

Global Sugar Art: www.globalsugarart.com

Shop Bakers Nook: www.shopbakersnook.com

Wilton: www.wilton.com

Star of David Sugar Toppers

Shop Bakers Nook: www.shopbakersnook.com

Craft Stores

Regional craft stores usually carry a variety of supplies, sprinkles, food coloring mist, candy eyes, candy coating, food coloring, and so on.

Hobby Lobby: www.hobbylobby.com

Jo-Ann Fabric and Craft Stores: www.joann.com

Michaels: www.michaels.com

Tools

These are my must-have tools and they can be found at any grocery or craft store, but you probably already have most of them.

- Kitchen shears
- Toothpicks
- Small knife
- Edible markers
- Parchment or wax paper
- Food-safe paintbrush
- Fondant roller
- Cookie cutters
- Lollipop sticks

Tips & Tricks

Halloween

Cute Pumpkin Donuts

Sweet little donuts that are too cute to spook. These mini store-bought donuts are all dressed up for Halloween!

Makes 12 Cute Pumpkin Donuts

orange food coloring (optional)
1 (16-oz.) can vanilla frosting
12 mini donuts
orange sugar sprinkles
24 black nonpareil sprinkles
12 bat-shaped Halloween sprinkles or 6 black, round sprinkles, cut in half
12 Tootsie Rolls
4 green gumdrops

1. Squeeze a few drops of orange coloring into the can of vanilla frosting and stir to incorporate.
2. Frost the mini donuts with the orange frosting. Immediately shake the orange sugar sprinkles on the frosting. It is helpful to have a bowl underneath so you can reuse the leftover sprinkles.
3. Push 2 black nonpareil sprinkles into the side of the donut for eyes.
4. With a toothpick dipped in frosting, attach the black bat sprinkle upside down on the donut for the mouth.
5. Place a Tootsie Roll in the center of the donut for the stem.
6. Using a small knife, cut a small leaf shape from a green gumdrop and attach with frosting to the stem.

Full Moon Cupcakes

The little graveyard scene on these cupcakes will really lift your spirits! Yummy chocolate cupcakes topped with a lollipop moon that lights the way for some eensy weensy white chocolate chip ghosts.

Makes 12 Full Moon Cupcakes

12 Oreos

12 store-bought unfrosted chocolate cupcakes

1 (16-oz.) can chocolate frosting

36 white chocolate chips

black edible marker

12 yellow lollipops

Picket fence cupcake wrapper made by Wilton can be found online or at Michael's.

1. Using a food processor or a rolling pin and plastic zipper bag, finely crush the cookies.

2. Spread the chocolate frosting on the top of each cupcake.

3. Sprinkle the crushed cookies on top of the frosting.

4. With a black edible marker, make 2 eyes and a mouth on the white chocolate chips for the ghosts. Place them on top of the cupcakes.

5. Draw small bats on the yellow lollipops and push them into the cupcakes.

Black Cat Oreos

For when you're "feline" spooky. You'll be glad this cute and easy treat made from Oreos crossed your path!

Makes 12 Black Cat Oreos

1 (16-oz.) can chocolate frosting

24 green M&M's

black edible marker

**12 orange pumpkin sprinkles
or circle sprinkles**

24 chocolate chips

12 Oreos

1. Frost the back of 2 green M&M's and place them on top of an Oreo.
2. Using the black edible marker, draw eyes in the middle of the M&M's.
3. With a toothpick dipped in the frosting, attach a pumpkin sprinkle upside down to the cookie for the nose.
4. Dip the flat part of 2 chocolate chips in the frosting and attach to the top of the Oreo for the ears.

Norene Cox

Marshmallow Pie Bats

They're bat-tastic. Put some of these yummy marshmallow bats in your belfry. A sweet Halloween treat so cute, everyone will go batty over it!

𝑀𝑎𝑘𝑒𝑠 12 Marshmallow Pie Bats

1 (16-oz.) can chocolate frosting
24 candy eyes
12 chocolate marshmallow pies
black licorice lace
6 mini marshmallows
6 chocolate wafer cookies

1. Spread a small amount of frosting on the back of 2 candy eyes and place them on the marshmallow pie.
2. Cut approximately 3 inches of black licorice lace and attach it to the marshmallow pie with frosting for the mouth.
3. Using a knife, slice 2 small triangles from mini marshmallow and stick them to the underside of the mouth for fangs.
4. Cut a chocolate wafer cookie in half. Turn the halves upside down and push them into each side of the marshmallow pie for wings.

Graveyard Pudding Cups

So frightfully easy to make, it's scary. These pudding cups will soon disappear, since the kids will be "goblin" these up in no time. Perfect for classroom parties!

Makes 12 Graveyard Pudding Cups

12 Oreo cookies
12 chocolate pudding cups
12 Peeps ghosts
12 pumpkin candies

1. Using a food processor or a rolling pin and plastic zipper bag, finely crush the cookies.
2. Open up the pudding cups and sprinkle the crushed cookies on top.
3. Place a Peeps ghost and candy pumpkin in each cup.
4. That's it. You're done. Really, I mean it.

Rice Krispies Halloween Treat Bags

No tricks in this bag, just a bag full of treats! Fill this Rice Krispies Treat up with candy and you've got yourself one spooktacular snack.

Makes 6 Rice Krispies Halloween Treat Bags

6 cherry-orange Fruit Roll-Ups

6 store-bought Rice Krispies Treats

black edible marker

1 (16-oz.) can vanilla frosting

variety of small candies: jelly beans, M&M's, Halloween candy, etc.

black licorice lace

1. Using kitchen shears, cut a strip of the cherry-orange Fruit Roll-Up and wrap it around the Rice Krispies Treat. Trim with kitchen shears to fit.

2. Write "Trick or Treat" on the front of the treat with a black edible marker.

3. Lightly frost the top of the treat and add small candies.

4. Cut approximately 2 inches of the black licorice lace and push each end into the top of the treat for the handle.

Skeleton Grahams

No bones about it, these are so easy to make! Chocolate graham crackers and marshmallows make this edible craft so fun, it'll tickle your funny bone.

Makes 12 Skeleton Grahams

6 regular-size marshmallows

black edible marker

approximately ½ cup chocolate candy coating wafers

12 graham crackers

36 peppermint Tic Tac candies

48 bone-shaped candies

24 white jimmie sprinkles

1. Using kitchen shears or a knife dipped in water, cut the marshmallow in half horizontally.

2. On the smooth, flat part of the marshmallow, make 2 dots for the eyes and draw in a smile with vertical lines for the mouth with a black edible marker.

3. Melt the candy coating according to the package directions. Secure the marshmallow head to the graham cracker with the melted candy coating.

4. Using a toothpick dipped in melted candy coating, attach 3 Tic Tac candies horizontally underneath the marshmallow head.

5. Attach the bone candies and white jimmies sprinkles for the skeleton arms and legs and feet with a toothpick dipped in candy coating.

Meringue Ghost Cupcakes

Boo-tifully simple cupcakes. Store-bought meringue cookies make these cupcakes so easy, it's a scream.

Makes 12 Meringue Ghost Cupcakes

12 vanilla meringue cookies
black edible marker
12 cupcakes, frosted white

1. Using a black edible marker, draw 2 small ovals for the eyes and a large oval for the mouth on each meringue cookie.
2. Place the meringue cookies on top of the cupcakes.

Norene Cox

Werewolf Peanut Butter Cups

You'll have a howling good time making these fang-tastic treats. These werewolves are made from everyone's favorite candy—peanut butter cups. So watch out! Having to share these frightfully good treats could get a little hairy.

Makes 12 Werewolf Peanut Putter Cups

1 (16-oz.) can chocolate frosting
12 peanut butter cups
chocolate jimmie sprinkles
24 red M&M's
black edible marker
12 small black jelly beans
24 mini marshmallows
24 chocolate chips

1. Spread the chocolate frosting on top of the peanut butter cups.
2. Sprinkle on the chocolate jimmies and gently press them on top of the frosted peanut butter cups.
3. With the black edible maker, draw the eyes in the middle of 2 red M&M's and attach them to each peanut butter cup with frosting.
4. Using a small amount of frosting, attach a black jelly bean in the middle of the peanut butter cup for the nose.
5. Cut 4 small triangles from mini marshmallows. It may help to dip the knife in warm water to prevent sticking. Attach the small marshmallow triangles to the top of the peanut butter cup with a toothpick dipped in frosting.
6. Attach 2 chocolate chips for ears, using chocolate frosting to the top of the cookie.

Crow-eos

Perfect to dunk in your caw-fee. Yummy crow cookies made from Oreos and circus peanuts.

Makes 12 Crow-eos

12 orange circus peanut candies
24 candy eyes
12 Oreo cookies
1 (16-oz.) can chocolate frosting
black licorice lace

1. Using a small knife or kitchen shears, cut a teardrop shape out of the circus peanut for the beak. Flatten it a little with your fingers.
2. Attach the beak and 2 candy eyes to the Oreo cookie with chocolate frosting.
3. Cut small strands of black licorice lace approximately ½-inch long and tuck 3 pieces into the cream filling at the top of each Oreo.

Marshmallow Frankies

A monstrously fun way to transform your marshmallows into Halloween treats. A silly snack for all little ghouls and boys.

Makes 24 Marshmallow Frankies

green candy coating
24 lollipop sticks
24 regular marshmallows
black sugar sprinkles
black edible marker
styrofoam block

1. Melt the green candy coating according to the package instructions.
2. Push a lollipop stick into the bottom of a marshmallow.
3. Dip a marshmallow into the candy coating and tap it the side of the bowl with the stick to remove excess candy coating.
4. Dip the top of the marshmallow into the black sprinkles.
5. Place the stick into a Styrofoam block to dry completely.
6. Using a black edible marker, draw on a Frankie face.
7. Carefully pull off the lollipop stick (or leave it on for a Frankie Marshmallow Pop).

Mummy Spoons

Perfect for hot cocoa on Halloween night, or for your coffin break. Watch your mummy melt away in a cup of hot chocolate after a fun night of trick-or-treating!

𝓜𝓪𝓴𝓮𝓼 15 Mummy Spoons

15 plastic spoons

1 (12-oz.) bag white candy coating wafers

30 mini M&M's

1. Melt candy coating according to package instructions.
2. Scoop candy coating into the spoon so it is evenly coated.
3. Place on parchment paper.
4. Pour some of the candy coating into a plastic zipper bag.
5. Cut off one small corner of the bottom of the bag and pipe the candy coating back and forth horizontally across the top of the spoons.
6. Place the mini M&M's on the spoons for the eyes. Let dry completely.
7. Great all wrapped up for a party favor too!

Spider Marshmallow Pops

A sweet little spin on marshmallows. This creepy crawly marshmallow snack is the perfect bite!

Makes 12 Spider Marshmallow Pops

1 (.75-oz.) black decorating gel tube

12 regular size marshmallows

approximately ½ cup white candy coating wafers

24 black M&M's

black edible marker

12 lollipop sticks

black sugar sprinkles

1. Using the black decorating gel, pipe a spiral starting from the inside of the marshmallow top until you get to the edge.
2. Starting from the center of the swirl, lightly drag a toothpick in a straight line to the edge. Repeat this step around the marshmallow and you will get a web.
3. Melt the white candy coating according to the package instructions.
4. With a toothpick dipped in melted candy coating, attach 2 M&M's to the side of the marshmallow.
5. Draw 8 legs with a black edible marker around each M&M for the spiders.
6. Push a lollipop stick in the middle of the web on top of the marshmallow.
7. Holding the lollipop stick, dip the bottom of the marshmallow in the melted candy coating.
8. Immediately dip the bottom of the marshmallow into the black sugar sprinkles.
9. Place on parchment or wax paper to dry.

Thanksgiving

Teeny Tiny Turkey Tables

Feast your eyes on the cutest Thanksgiving treat ever. A graham cracker table topped with a dinky dinner. So cute that kids will giggle and women will squeal. You know you want to make these.

Makes 4 Teeny Tiny Turkey Tables

32 almond slices

80 green jimmie sprinkles

16 white Necco Wafer candies

1 (16-oz.) can white frosting

1 (.75-oz.) tube yellow decorating gel

4 graham crackers

4 pumpkin candies

autumn leaves sprinkles

8 wafer cookies

TIP

If making this treat in advance, do NOT attach the table legs until right before serving or the table will sag and buckle in the middle. Trust me, I had itty bitty broken tables overnight.

1. Attach 2 almond slices and 5 green jimmies to a white Necco Wafer using a toothpick dipped in frosting.

2. Place a small dollop of frosting on the Necco Wafer to resemble mashed potatoes.

3. Carefully squeeze a little yellow gel icing into the middle of the mashed potato frosting.

4. Secure the 4 Necco plates to the graham cracker with frosting.

5. Frost underneath the pumpkin candy and place it in the middle of the graham cracker.

6. Spread a thin layer of frosting around the pumpkin and press the autumn leaves sprinkles in the frosting.

7. Frost one long edge on 2 of the wafer cookies. Attach the frosted side of the wafer cookie to the underside of the graham cracker on each end.

Pilgrim Truffle Cookies

A pair of Pilgrims so sweet you'll be thankful you made them. combine white truffles with marshmallow cookies and you have a delicious little duo.

Makes 1 pilgrim couple

2 white chocolate truffles

black edible marker

1 white Airhead candy

approximately ½ cup white candy coating wafers

1 vanilla wafer cookie

1 Rolo candy

1 (.68-oz.) white writing icing tube (not gel icing)

1 yellow confetti sprinkle

2 chocolate covered marshmallow cookies

1 white jumbo heart sprinkle

1. Draw smiley faces on each white chocolate truffle.

2. Using a knife or kitchen shears, cut off 2 inches of the white Airhead candy.

3. Wrap the 2-inch Airhead candy around a white chocolate truffle for the lady pilgrim's hat to frame her face. Pinch the back of the hat a little to give it a bonnet shape.

4. Melt the white candy coating wafers according to the package instructions.

5. Dip the bottom of the lady pilgrim head into the melted candy coating and attach to the top of the chocolate-covered marshmallow cookie.

6. Using a toothpick dipped in melted candy coating, attach the jumbo heart sprinkle to the front of the marshmallow cookie.

7. Spread a little melted candy coating on the top of the pilgrim man's head. Place the vanilla wafer on top and let it dry.

8. Dip the bottom of the Rolo candy into the melted candy coating and place it in the middle of the vanilla wafer.

9. Pipe a line of icing, using the white icing writing tube around the bottom of the Rolo candy. Place a round yellow confetti sprinkle in the front-middle of the icing band.

10. Dip the bottom of the pilgrim man's head into them melted candy coating and attach it to the top of the chocolate-covered marshmallow cookie.

Pilgrim Hat Brownies

Buckle up for these mint chocolate treats. Peppermint patties topped with bite-size brownies make an amazing dessert you'll be sure to tip your hat to.

Makes 12 Pilgrim Hat Brownies

12 mini brownie bites

12 regular-sized York Peppermint Patties

1 (7-oz.) pouch black cookie icing

12 yellow Chiclet gum pieces

1. Using the black cookie icing, squeeze a dime-sized amount of icing on the top of a mini brownie.
2. Place the brownie icing side-down in the middle of a York Peppermint Pattie.
3. Pipe a band of black cookie icing around the brownie to make the hat band.
4. Place a yellow Chiclet gum piece in the middle of the band.

Caramel Ginger Turkeys

Your guests will love these gingersnap turkeys. Make a flock of these turkey cookies because they will be gobbled up in a snap!

Makes 12 Caramel Ginger Turkeys

24 black nonpareil
12 individually-wrapped caramels
12 orange mini chip sprinkles
12 red heart sprinkles
1 (16-oz.) can chocolate frosting
12 gingersnap cookies
60 pieces candy corn
24 orange leaf sprinkles

1. Push 2 black nonpareil sprinkles in a caramel for the eyes.
2. Using a toothpick dipped in chocolate frosting, attach an orange mini chip in the middle of the caramel for the beak.
3. Attach a red heart upside down under the beak for the wattle with frosting.
4. Spread frosting on the back of the caramel and place it on top of a gingersnap cookie.
5. Frost one side of a candy corn and place it on the cookie with the point-side facing the caramel. Repeat with the other 4 candy corns and arrange them around the caramel on the cookie so they look like feathers.

Norene Cox

Turkey Pudding Cups

Gobble 'til you wobble. Children will love creating these quirky little turkey pudding cups!

Makes 4 Turkey Pudding Cups

¼ **cup chocolate candy coating wafers**

8 **candy eyes**

4 **Milano cookies**

4 **candy corn**

4 **red heart sprinkles**

4 **chocolate snack pudding cups**

1 **(5-oz.) bag assorted Swedish Fish candy**

1. Melt the candy coating according to the package instructions.
2. With a toothpick dipped in melted candy coating, secure the candy eyes to a Milano cookie.
3. Cut off the tip of a candy corn for the beak. Attach to the cookie with melted candy coating under the eyes.
4. Turn the red heart sprinkle upside down and, using a toothpick dipped in melted candy coating, place the upside-down heart under the beak for the wattle.
5. Open up a pudding cup and push a cookie into the middle of the pudding cup.
6. Arrange 5 Swedish fish candies in an assortment of colors, tail-side down behind the cookie for the feathers.

Pilgrim Donut Ships

Nothing but smooth sailing when making these dessert donuts. Donuts adorned with pretzels, Fruit Roll-Ups, and a paper sail will take you into a whole new world.

Makes 6 Pilgrim Donut Ships

white paper
6 pretzel sticks
1 red Fruit Roll-Up
6 chocolate mini donuts

1. Cut a 1½-inch trapezoid out of white paper for the sail.
2. Bend (don't fold) the sail vertically and cut 2 small slits in the middle, one near the top of the sail and one near the bottom.
3. Thread a pretzel stick through the slits.
4. Push the bottom of the pretzel sail into the top edge of the donut.
5. Using kitchen shears, cut a small triangle out of the red Fruit Roll-Up for the flag. Press it to the top of the pretzel to make it stick. You may use a small amount of water to secure it if needed.

Mini Pie Cookies

There won't be any leftovers when it comes to these mini desserts! If your little ones don't like pumpkin pie, they can still have a slice of fun with these treats made from vanilla wafers!

Makes 12 Mini Pie Cookies

12 mini vanilla wafers
6 individually wrapped caramels
¼ cup white candy coating wafers
12 snowflake sprinkles

1. Unwrap a caramel and place it on a microwave-safe plate.
2. Microwave for approximately 5 seconds until it is soft and easy to mold.
3. Divide the caramel in half.
4. Roll half of the caramel into a ball. Then place it on parchment or wax paper and roll it out into a long rope.
5. Wrap the rope around the edges of the mini vanilla wafer for the crust. Trim it with a knife to fit.
6. With the side of a toothpick, make crimps around the edges of the caramel crust.
7. Melt the candy coating according to the package directions.
8. Using a toothpick dipped in melted candy coating, attach a snowflake sprinkle to the center of the cookie.

Sugar Daddy Turkeys

Nothing could be sweeter than these super easy-to-make caramel creations for Thanksgiving!

Makes 8 Sugar Daddy Turkeys

¼ cup white candy coating wafers

16 candy eyes

8 Sugar Daddy candy pops

8 candy corns

8 jumbo heart sprinkles

1. Melt the candy coating wafers according to the package instructions

2. With a toothpick dipped in the melted candy coating, attach 2 candy eyes to the Sugar Daddy pop.

3. Cut the tip off a candy corn for the beak. Attach it to the Sugar Daddy under the eyes for the beak.

4. For the wattle, turn the jumbo heart sprinkle upside down and secure it to the Sugar Daddy under the beak.

Marshmallow Pumpkin Pie Cupcakes

A cupcake to pie for. Top your Thanksgiving cupcakes with a slice of marshmallow cuteness that really tastes like pumpkin pie!

Makes 6 Marshmallow Pumpkin Pie Cupcakes

6 Jet-Puffed Pumpkin Spice marshmallows*

6 individually wrapped caramels

6 vanilla Mallow Bits

6 frosted cupcakes

1. Using a knife, cut a small piece from a Pumpkin Spice marshmallow to resemble a slice of pie. (It is easier to cut marshmallows with a wet knife.)
2. Unwrap a caramel and place on a microwave-safe plate. Microwave the caramel for approximately 5 seconds to soften.
3. Press the caramel flat or use a fondant roller to roll it flat.
4. Place the cut marshmallow on top of the flattened caramel and using a knife, cut the caramel around the marshmallow, leaving enough to fold up the back of the pie slice to resemble crust. Trim to fit.
5. Place a vanilla Mallow Bit on top.
6. Put the "pie" on top of a frosted cupcake.

TIP

If you have trouble finding the pumpkin spice marshmallows, a good substitution would be the orange circus peanut candies.

Rice Krispies Treat Dreidels

A fun spin on dessert! Turn a Rice Krispies Treat into a delicious dreidel!

Makes 4 Rice Krispies Treat Dreidels

4 store-bought Rice Krispies Treat bars

1 (12-oz.) pkg. blue candy coating wafers

½ cup white candy coating wafers

4 pretzel sticks

white rolled fondant

Star of David sugar decorations

1. Cut the corners off one end of a Rice Krispies Treat bar into a "V" shape for the dreidel point.
2. Melt the blue candy coating wafers according to the package instructions.
3. Using a fork, fully immerse the Rice Krispies Treat into the melted blue candy coating. Tap the side of the bowl with the fork to remove any excess candy coating. Place on parchment or wax paper to set.
4. Melt the white candy coating wafers according to the package instructions.
5. Dip in the pretzel stick and tap it on the side of the bowl to remove any excess candy coating. Place on parchment or wax paper to dry.
6. Roll out the white fondant and trim it to fit the top of the Rice Krispies Treat.
7. Using the melted white candy coating, attach the Star of David sugar decoration to the top of the Rice Krispies Treat.
8. Push the pretzel into the flat end of the Rice Krispies Treat.

Mini Menorahs

Candy candles and delicious donuts make this dessert divine! Make an edible Festival of Lights centerpiece for the children's table.

Makes 1 Mini Menorah

10 mini powdered donuts
1 (16-oz.) can vanilla frosting
blue food coloring
silver dragées
9 blue candy canes
9 mini yellow mint chips

1. Stir in a few drops of blue food coloring into the can of vanilla frosting until it is incorporated and the desired blue color is achieved.
2. Using a knife or a 1M swirl Wilton decorating tip, frost the tops of 9 powdered sugar donuts. Attach one of the frosted donuts on top of another with frosting and place them in the center of the platter.
3. Sprinkle with silver dragées.
4. Place 4 donuts on each side of the middle donut.
5. Using a small knife, cut the candy canes at the curve.
6. Push a candy cane stick in the center of each donut.
7. Attach the yellow mint chips to the top of each candy cane stick with frosting.

Oreo Gelt Cookies

Shimmering chocolate cookies for your Hanukkah celebration. Topped with chocolate gelt, these cookies will make your celebration shine!

Makes 4 Oreo Gelt Cookies

1 (12-oz.) bag or 1 (16-oz.) bark white candy coating

12 Oreo cookies

1 (1.5-oz.) can silver food coloring mist

12 chocolate gelt

1. Melt the candy coating according to the package instructions.
2. Using a fork, dip the Oreo into the melted candy coating. Tap the fork on the side of the bowl to remove any excess.
3. Carefully slide the Oreo onto parchment paper. Let it dry completely.
4. Spray the coated Oreo with the silver food coloring mist. Place chocolate gelt in the middle of the Oreo.

Cute Hanukkah Cake Bites

These sweet petite squares for Hanukkah take the cake for cuteness! Sparkling blue sugar sprinkles easily dress up small bites of pound cake.

Makes approximately 30 cake squares

1 (10.75-oz.) pkg. frozen pound cake
1 (16-oz.) can vanilla frosting
blue sugar sprinkles
white Necco Wafer candies
blue edible marker

1. Cut pound cake into ½-inch slices.
2. Trimming the crust, cut the slices into 2-inch squares.
3. Frost the tops of each square and immediately dip them into a bowl of blue sugar sprinkles.
4. Using a blue edible marker, draw a Star of David or Menorah on a white Necco Wafer candy.
5. Attach the decorated Necco Wafer to the top of the cake with frosting.

Dreidel Meringue Pops

Everyone wins with these cute sugary spins. A fun-to-eat marshmallow treat that really does spin!

Makes 12 Dreidel Meringue Pops

½ cup white candy coating wafers

12 mini meringue cookies

12 regular size marshmallows

1 (1.5-oz.) can blue food coloring mist

blue edible marker

6 lollipop sticks

1. Melt the white candy coating wafers according to the package instructions.
2. Attach a mini meringue cookie to the top of the marshmallow with the melted candy coating.
3. Spray the marshmallow and meringue with blue food coloring mist. Let dry.
4. Draw the Hebrew letters for the dreidel on the sides of the marshmallows.
5. Cut a lollipop stick in half.
6. Push a lollipop stick half into the end of the marshmallow.

Winter Wonderland

Snowman Marshmallow Pops

These little guys will melt your heart and keep you warm at the same time. Simple treats the kiddos can make on a snowy afternoon!

Makes 12 Snowman Marshmallow Pops

black edible marker
12 regular marshmallows
**12 orange candy coated
     sunflower seeds**
12 lollipop sticks
12 regular size Oreos
1 (16-oz.) can white frosting
12 Rolo candies
12 large blue snowflake sprinkles
12 small white snowflake sprinkles

1. Using the black edible marker, make two dots for eyes on the flat round end of a marshmallow.
2. Make 6 dots for the mouth with the black edible marker.
3. Push the blunt end of the orange sunflower seed into the marshmallow for the nose. It may be helpful to make a small hole first with a toothpick.
4. Push a lollipop stick into the bottom of the marshmallow.
5. Separate an Oreo cookie and use the part without the filling. Frost the top of the marshmallow and place the cookie part of the Oreo on top.
6. Place a little bit of frosting on the top of a Rolo candy and attach it upside down on top of the Oreo cookie.
7. Using a small amount of frosting on a toothpick, secure the snowflake sprinkles to the Oreo hat.

Meringue Cookie Christmas Trees

Sweet little trees to light up your holiday. Light and airy cookies to top your favorite cupcakes or, in my case, yummy white chocolate peanut butter cups!

Makes 4 Meringue Cookie Christmas Trees

8 small store-bought meringue cookies

green food coloring mist

1 (16-oz.) can white frosting or melted white chocolate

Pastel confetti sprinkles

4 white Reese's Peanut Butter Cups or 4 cupcakes, frosted white

1. Place the meringue cookies on parchment paper and lightly spray them with the food color mist. Let dry completely.
2. Slice a small piece off the top of a cookie so it is flat. Attach another cookie on top with a little bit of white frosting or melted white chocolate.
3. Using a toothpick dipped in frosting or white chocolate, make small dots on the tree and place confetti sprinkles on top.
4. Place your tree on a cupcake or white chocolate peanut butter cup.

Hot Cocoa Marshmallow Cookies

Martha approved. I'm not even kidding. It's kind of surreal when Martha Stewart actually says what you made is "adorable." My hot cocoa marshmallow mug cookies won her over and believe me, it is "a good thing."

Makes 4 Hot Cocoa Marshmallow Cookies

approximately ¼ cup white candy coating

4 mini candy canes

4 large marshmallows

1 (16-oz.) can chocolate frosting

12 Jet-Puffed Mallow Bits

1 (7-oz.) pouch store-bought white cookie icing

4 store-bought tea cookies

40 small tree sprinkles

4 large tree sprinkles

1. Melt the candy coating in a small microwave-safe bowl according to the package instructions.
2. Cut a candy cane at the curve. Dip the ends into the melted candy coating and push them into side of marshmallow. Hold it in place until it hardens and is secure.
3. Using a small knife, spread a small amount of chocolate frosting on top of a marshmallow, leaving a small rim. Top with 3 Mallow Bits.
4. Frost a cookie with white icing. Place the marshmallow in the middle of the cookie.
5. Place 10 small tree sprinkles around the perimeter of the cookie.
6. Attach a large tree sprinkle to the front of the marshmallow using the candy coating.

Winter Sparkle Cupcakes

Store-bought cupcakes all glammed up for a winter gala. Brighten up your holiday and turn ordinary cupcakes into a winter wonderland!

Makes 12 Winter Sparkle Cupcakes

approximately 6 oz. store-bought, ready-to-use white fondant

fondant roller

small daisy or star cookie cutter

multi-pastel dragées

12 store-bought cupcakes with white frosting

1. Using a fondant roller, roll out the white fondant ⅛-inch thick and cut out 12 daisy shapes with the cookie cutter.

2. Push a dragée into the fondant at each end of the daisy petals and one in the center. Let it dry overnight.

3. Sprinkle the top of the cupcakes with the dragées. Place a daisy upright in the middle of each cupcake.

Polar Bear Peanut Butter Cups

Unbearably creamy and cute, these bears will leave you feeling warm and fuzzy inside!

Makes 6 Polar Bear Peanut Butter Cups

1 (12-oz.) bag white candy coating wafers

12 mini black jelly beans

6 (1. 5 oz.) pkg. Reese's White Peanut Butter Cups

24 black pearl sprinkles

1. Reserve 36 candy coating wafers for the ears and snout. Melt the remaining wafers according to package instructions.

2. Slice off ¼ of a white candy coating wafer with a small knife.

3. Dip the sliced end of a white candy coating wafer into the melted candy coating. Press and hold onto the side of a peanut butter cup until secure.

4. Now do the same with another wafer to make a pair of ears.

5. Attach a candy coating wafer to the middle of the peanut butter cup for the snout, using the melted candy coating as the glue.

6. Using a toothpick dipped in melted candy coating, place a small drop of coating in the middle of the wafer snout. Place the jelly bean on top for the nose.

7. Attach 2 black pearl sprinkles for eyes, using a toothpick dipped in the melted candy coating.

Sweet Snowman Hats

Even Frosty would think these are pretty cool. These darling little derbies are made from mint patties and Junior Mints. So easy to create, these mini minty hats are a perfect little treat to pop in your mouth after dinner!

Makes 12 Sweet Snowman Hats

1 (7-oz.) store-bought white cookie icing pouch

12 small snack-size mint patties

12 Junior Mints

holly-shaped sprinkles

1. Squeeze a nickel-size amount of cookie icing in the middle of the small mint patty.
2. Push a Junior Mint on top of the icing until it forms a small ring around the bottom of the Junior Mint.
3. Place 1 holly berry sprinkle in the icing and 2 holly leaves on each side of the berry.

White Truffle Snowmen

Almost too cute to eat… almost. Made from white chocolate truffles, this little guy will disappear faster than a snowball in the summertime. He makes a cute cupcake topper too!

Makes 1 White Truffle Snowman

approximately ¼ cup white candy coating wafers

2 white chocolate truffles

1 orange chip sprinkle

black edible marker

approximately ¼ cup blue candy coating wafers

blue jumbo round sprinkles

small white snowflake sprinkles

blue confetti sprinkles

blue Fruit Roll-Up

1. Melt the white candy coating according to the package instructions.
2. Dip the end of one truffle into the candy coating and place the other truffle on top. Hold until set.
3. Using a toothpick dipped in candy coating, place a small dot in the center of the top truffle and attach the orange chip sprinkle for the nose.
4. With a black edible marker, make 2 dots for the eyes on the truffle and 6 dots for the mouth.
5. Melt the blue candy coating according to package instructions. With a toothpick dipped in the blue candy coating, draw a line on top of the snowman's head.
6. Attach 2 blue jumbo confetti sprinkles with the melted candy coating at each end of the line for earmuffs.
7. With a toothpick dipped in candy coating, place a dot on top of each earmuff and attach a snowflake sprinkle.
8. Next, using the candy coating, attach small blue confetti sprinkles to the bottom truffle for buttons.
9. Using kitchen shears, cut out a small thin strip of the blue Fruit Roll-Up and tie it around the neck of the snowman.

Norene Cox

Santa Claus Is Coming to Town

Krispie Kringles

Jolly Old St. Nick Rice Krispies Treats. These treats have Santa sporting a sugary cap and a beard made of sweet coconut.

Makes 16 Krispie Kringles

1 (12-oz.) bag white candy coating

16 store-bought Rice Krispies Treats

red sugar sprinkles

16 white Sixlet candies

1 cup shredded coconut

32 candy eyes

16 red cinnamon imperial candies

1. Melt the white candy coating according to the package instructions.
2. Dip both ends of the Rice Krispies Treat into the melted candy coating. Place on parchment paper.
3. Sprinkle the red sugar sprinkles on top of the melted candy coating at one end, leaving a line of white candy coating for the brim of the hat.
4. Place a white Sixlet candy in the corner for the pom on the hat.
5. Sprinkle the shredded coconut over the melted candy coating on the other end of the Rice Krispies Treat.
6. Dip the back of 2 candy eyes into the melted candy coating and place in the middle of the treat.
7. Attach a cinnamon candy with the melted candy coating for a nose.

Oreo Ornaments

Decking the halls never looked so yummy. Get crafty and let your imagination run wild when decorating these sweet ornaments!

Makes 12 Oreo Ornaments

1 (12-oz.) bag or 1 (16-oz.) bark white candy coating

12 Oreo cookies

12 yellow Dot candies

assorted sprinkles and Fruit Roll-Ups

1. Melt the candy coating according to the package instructions.
2. Using a fork, dip the Oreos one at a time into the melted candy coating. Tap the fork on the side of the bowl to remove excess.
3. Carefully slide the Oreo onto parchment paper.
4. Place a Dot candy on the top side of the Oreo.
5. Add sprinkles or cut out shapes from the Fruit Roll-Ups using small cookie cutters to decorate.

Santa's Sugary Sleds

It's sledgendary. Pile on the presents made of all things sweet to make this edible sled!

Makes 1 Santa's Sugary Sled

4 wafer cookies

1 (16-oz.) can white frosting

2 mini candy canes

2 jumbo star sprinkles

Starburst and Jolly Rancher Chew candies

1 (.68-oz.) white writing icing tube (not gel icing)

1 green Life Saver candy

heart, red confetti, and pearl sprinkles

1. Place 2 wafer cookies side by side and adhere them together with frosting.
2. Frost the tops and place 2 cookies side by side on top.
3. Attach a mini candy cane and a star sprinkle to each side of the sled with frosting.
4. Spread a little frosting on the back of the sled and put the Starburst and Jolly Rancher candies on top for the presents.
5. Using the writing icing tube, make ribbons on the presents and top with heart and confetti sprinkles for bows.
6. Frost the back of the green Life Saver candy and place it on the front of the sled.
7. Using a toothpick dipped in frosting, attach red confetti sprinkles around the wreath and 2 hearts with the ends pointing together as the bow.

Norene Cox

Pretty Presents

Give the gift of yummy goodness. Wrap up some treats with Fruit Roll-Ups and sprinkle bows. So easy to make, it's like a present in itself!

Makes 8 Pretty Presents

6 store-bought Rice Krispies Treats

6 Fruit Roll-Ups in a variety of colors

variety of sprinkles

white frosting or white candy coating (optional)

red licorice lace

1. Cut the Rice Krispies Treats into desired shapes with a knife.
2. Wrap the treats with Fruit Roll-Ups and trim the excess using kitchen shears.
3. Decorate with sprinkles. They should stick to the Fruit Roll-Up just fine, or you can dip a toothpick in frosting or melted candy coating and attach the sprinkles to make them more secure.
4. Cut a small 2-inch piece of licorice lace and push it into the top of a treat for a gift bag handle.

Santa's Big Belly Sugar Cookies

Get in mah belly. Leave these cookies for the big guy and he'll surely put you on the nice list.

Makes 12 Santa's Big Belly Sugar Cookies

12 store-bought sugar cookies
1 (7-oz.) pouch red cookie icing
12 yellow Starburst candies
12 black licorice vines
black edible marker

1. Turn a cookie over to work on a flat surface.
2. Using the red cookie icing pouch, squeeze a circle of icing around the cookie.
3. Fill in the rest of the cookie with icing.
4. While the icing is soft, place a yellow Starburst in the middle of the cookie for the buckle.
5. Cut the black licorice with kitchen shears to fit on each side of the buckle. Place the licorice on each side of the buckle.
6. Let dry completely.
7. With a black edible marker, make a small square in the middle of the yellow Starburst to resemble a buckle.

Christmas Treat Trees

Trim a tasty tree treat. Rice Krispies Treats decorated with frosting and sprinkles make festive little trees that are sure to please!

Makes 8 Christmas Treat Trees

8 store-bought Rice Krispies Treats
green food coloring
1 (16-oz.) can white frosting
confetti sprinkles
8 yellow jumbo star sprinkles
8 mini candy canes

1. Using a knife, cut the Rice Krispies Treat into a tall triangle to resemble a tree.
2. Put a few drops of green food coloring into the can of vanilla frosting and stir to incorporate. You can add more food coloring to get the green color you desire.
3. Spread the frosting on top of the treat.
4. Place the confetti sprinkles on the frosting to decorate.
5. Top the tree with a yellow jumbo star sprinkle.
6. Cut the mini candy canes at the curve.
7. Push the straight end of a candy cane into the bottom of the tree for the trunk.

The Sweet Express Trains

Chugga chugga chew chew! All aboard for a freight-load of fun! Sweeter than any toy in Santa's workshop, this train treat is on the right track for a good time.

Makes 4 The Sweet Express Trains

½ **cup chocolate candy coating**
16 chocolate wafer cookies
8 red Life Saver candies
8 green Life Saver candies
16 starlight mints
12 jumbo tree sprinkles
16 small tree sprinkles

1. Melt the chocolate candy coating according to the package instructions.
2. Frost the top of a wafer cookie with the melted chocolate and place another wafer cookie on top for the base.
3. Cut a wafer cookie in half and attach the halves with the melted chocolate for the cab.
4. Attach the cab to the top of the base on one side.
5. Cut another wafer cookie in half and attach it to the top of the cab with melted chocolate.
6. Alternate the red and green Life Savers and attach them to each other with the melted chocolate for the engine.
7. Attach the engine with the melted chocolate to the base in front of the cab.
8. Place the melted chocolate on one side of the starlight mints and attach them to the base as wheels.
9. Using a toothpick dipped in the melted chocolate, attach a jumbo tree sprinkle to the end of the engine and one on each side of the cab.
10. Secure the small trees in the center of the wheels with a toothpick dipped in melted chocolate.

North Pole Ice Cream Sammies

It is super simple to make a stack of these festive sammies! Rolled in crushed mint candies, these mini ice cream sandwiches are mitten-lickin' good.

Makes 18 North Pole Ice Cream Sammies

1 (12-oz.) bag peppermint starlight mints

1 (12-oz.) bag spearmint starlight mints

18 mini ice cream sandwiches*

1 can chocolate or white frosting

red, green, and brown mini M&M's

small snowflake sprinkles

TIP

*If mini ice cream sandwiches are unavailable in your area, simply use regular ice cream sandwiches and regular size red, green, brown, and white M&M's instead.

1. Using a food processor or a plastic zipper food bag and a rolling pin, finely crush the candy flavors separately.
2. Unwrap an ice cream sandwich and roll the ice cream edges in the crushed candy.
3. Wrap and place in freezer for at least 1 hour.
4. Using a toothpick, dot the back of the mini M&M's and sprinkles with frosting and place on the top of the ice cream sandwich in a tree or candy cane pattern.
5. Wrap and freeze until ready to serve.

Rice Krispies Treat Santa Hats

Brimming with sweetness. Yummy Santa hats that kids will love. Made with their favorite Rice Krispies Treats and Fruit Roll-Ups, it will turn anyone into a kid at Christmas!

Makes 4 Rice Krispies Treat Santa Hats

4 store-bought Rice Krispies Treats

4 red Fruit Roll-Ups

4 white Sixlet candies

1 (16-oz.) can white frosting

white nonpareil sprinkles

1. Cut a Rice Krispies Treat into a tall triangle.
2. Wrap with a red Fruit Roll-Up. Trim the edges and press them together to secure.
3. Spread a little white frosting around the bottom edge of the hat.
4. Dip the bottom of the hat into a small dish filled with the white nonpareil sprinkles, making sure the frosting is coated with them.
5. Press a white Sixlet candy on top of the hat. It should stick just fine, or you can secure it with a little bit of white frosting.

Letter to Santa Toaster Pastries

Write a sweet letter that Santa will love. Whether they have been naughty or nice, the kids will be excited to make these North Pole notes!

Makes 4 letters to Santa

4 toaster pastries

1 (7-oz.) pouch white cookie icing

1 red Fruit Roll-Up

4 jumbo heart sprinkles

4 jumbo tree sprinkles

red, green, and black edible markers

1. Flip the toaster pastry over and frost it with the cookie icing.
2. Cut a small square of the red Fruit Roll-Up for the stamp with kitchen shears. Place it in the upper right corner of the letter.
3. Using a toothpick dipped in melted candy coating, place a dot in the middle of the stamp and place a jumbo tree sprinkle on top.
4. Place a jumbo heart sprinkle in the left corner of the letter.
5. Let the icing dry for 24 hours.
6. Make a slash mark design with alternating red and green edible markers around the edges of the icing.
7. Address the letter in black edible marker to Santa Claus, North Pole.

Reindeer Games

Chocolate Reindeer Spoons

Cuteness and cocoa—there's no better way to warm up! Cocoa couldn't be more adorable with these adorable reindeer spoons. So easy to make, you will be able to create Santa's entire team in a Blitzen! They make great holiday gifts too!

Makes 24 Chocolate Reindeer Spoons

1 (12-oz.) bag or 1 (16-oz.) bark milk chocolate candy coating

24 plastic spoons

48 mini candy canes

48 candy eyes

24 red or brown M&M's

1. Melt the chocolate candy coating according to the package instructions.
2. With the plastic spoon, scoop up the melted candy coating and make sure you coat the back of the spoon. Allow the excess to drip off.
3. Place the spoon on top of two mini candy canes that are laid out on parchment paper for the antlers.
4. Place the candy eyes and a red or brown M&M nose on top of the chocolate spoon. Let dry.
5. Tie a small ribbon around the spoon if desired.

Rudolph Milanos

En-deer-ing little cookies. No need to "Donner" on your apron to make these adorable reindeer chocolate cookies. Store-bought cookies are the secret to making these easy vixens.

Makes 8 Rudolph Milanos

approximately ¼ cup white candy coating wafers

8 starlight mints

8 chocolate Milano Melts cookies

8 red M&M's

16 candy eyes

8 mini pretzels

8 Trolli Strawberry Puffs candies

8 white Sixlet candies

1. Melt the white candy coating according to the package instructions.
2. Dip one side of the starlight mint into the melted candy coating and attach it to the top end of the Milano cookie.
3. Using a toothpick dipped in melted candy coating, make a small dot in the center of the starlight mint and place a red M&M on top.
4. Attach the candy eyes on the top of the cookie using a toothpick dipped in the melted candy coating.
5. Cut a pretzel in half and snap off the rounded ends to make the antlers. Dip one end into the candy coating and place on one side of the gummy strawberry puff. Hold in place until set.
6. Repeat with the other antler on the other side of the gummy puff.
7. Attach the Sixlet candy to the top of the gummy puff using the melted candy coating.
8. Secure the hat with antlers to the cookie using the melted candy coating.

Prancer Pudding Pies

Elf friendly and Santa approved. So easy to make that even your littlest elf will have no trouble creating this fun dessert!

Makes 6 Prancer Pudding Pies

6 (3.25–oz.) chocolate snack pudding cups

6 ready-made mini graham cracker crusts

12 candy eyes

12 chocolate-covered pretzels

6 Cherry Sours candies

1. Scoop out the chocolate pudding into the pie crust.
2. Place 2 candy eyes in the center of the pie and a Cherry Sour for the nose.
3. Place the chocolate-covered pretzels at the top of the pie for the antlers.

Snowy White Reindeer Cookies

Even Santa's team dreams of a white Christmas. Creamy white candy-coated Oreos with a snowy sprinkling of sugar, these cookies are both pretty and cute.

Makes 12 Snowy White Reindeer Cookies

1 (12-oz.) bag or 1 (16-oz.) bark white candy coating

12 Oreos

24 black pearl sprinkles

12 red M&M's

clear sugar crystal sprinkles

24 pretzels

1. Melt the candy coating according to the package instructions.
2. Using a fork, dip the Oreos one at a time into the melted candy coating. Tap the fork on the side of the bowl to remove any excess.
3. Carefully slide the Oreo onto parchment paper.
4. Place 2 black pearl sprinkles on the Oreo for the eyes.
5. Put an M&M in the center of the Oreo for the nose.
6. Dip a pretzel into the melted candy coating using a fork and tap the fork on the side of the bowl to remove excess.
7. Immediately sprinkle the pretzels with clear sugar crystals to cover.
8. Let everything dry completely.
9. Cut the pretzels so they resemble antlers.
10. Attach to the top of the Oreo using the melted candy coating.

Kwanzaa

Rice Krispies Treat Kinaras

Light up a sweet treat for Kwanzaa. Celebrate Kwanzaa with a chocolate Kinara and colorful candles made of licorice.

Makes 1 Rice Krispies Treat Kinaras

½ **cup chocolate candy coating wafers**

4 store-bought Double Chocolate Chunk Rice Krispies Treat bars

8 miniature peanut butter cups

3 soft red licorice pieces

3 soft green licorice pieces

1 black licorice piece

7 small yellow jelly beans

1. Melt the chocolate candy coating according to the package instructions.

2. Frost a short end of a chocolate Rice Krispies Treat with the melted chocolate candy coating and attach it to another short end of a Treat bar. Continue to secure the bars in this manner until there are 4 bars attached together in a long horizontal line.

3. Spread the bottom of a miniature peanut butter cup with the candy coating and place it in the center of the Rice Krispies Treat Kinara (the candle holder).

4. Attach the remaining peanut butter cups to the Kinara with the melted candy coating by evenly spacing 3 peanut butter cups on each side of the peanut butter cup in the center.

5. With the melted chocolate candy coating, secure an additional peanut butter cup on top of the peanut butter cup in the center.

6. Cut all licorice into 3-inch pieces.

7. Dip the bottom of each licorice piece and place them on top of each miniature peanut butter cup. Hold in place until set, with the 3 red licorice pieces on the left, the black one in the center and the 3 green on the right.

8. With a toothpick dipped in the chocolate candy coating, attach one end of a yellow jelly bean on top of each licorice piece. Hold in place until set.

Muhindi Waffles

A crafty corn snack that's fun to make! Frozen waffles and candy make this a fun dessert for the kids to create.

Makes 4 Muhindi Waffles

4 frozen toaster waffles

½ cup peanut butter

1 cup harvest M&M's (red, brown, tan, and yellow M&M's)

4 popsicle sticks

4 yellow Fruit Roll-Ups

1. Toast the waffles according to the package instructions.
2. Using kitchen shears, cut the waffle in a long oval shape.
3. Spread the peanut butter on 1 side of the M&M's and attach them to the waffle.
4. Push a popsicle stick into the bottom of the waffle.
5. Cut the yellow Fruit Roll-Ups in long leaf shapes and wrap them around the bottom of the waffle and the popsicle stick.

Kwanzaa Unity Cups

Kids will love to craft an ice cream cone into this Unity Cup (Kikombe cha Umoja).

Makes 1 Kwanzaa Unity Cup

½ **cup chocolate candy coating wafers**

1 wafer-style ice cream cone

green sugar sprinkles

1 strawberry Fruit by the Foot

black edible marker

black and green confetti sprinkles

1 Pirouette cookie

1 striped fudge cookie

1. Melt the chocolate candy coating wafers according to the package instructions.

2. Dip the rim of the cone into the melted candy coating and then immediately dip it into a shallow dish filled with green sugar sprinkles. Let dry.

3. Wrap the strawberry Fruit by the Foot around the cone just underneath the rim. Trim with kitchen shears to fit and secure ends with a dot of melted candy coating.

4. Draw a fun design on the Fruit by the Foot using a black edible marker.

5. With a toothpick dipped in melted chocolate candy coating, attach the confetti sprinkles around the drawn pattern in alternating black and green colors.

6. Using a small knife, cut off a 3-inch piece of the Pirouette cookie.

7. Dip one end of the cookie into the melted chocolate candy coating.

8. Place the bottom center of the ice cream cone on top of the candy coated end of the Pirouette cookie. Hold to set.

9. Dip the other end of the Pirouette cookie in the melted candy coating and place in the center of the fudge striped cookie. Hold in place to set.

New Year's Party

Midnight Marshmallow Pops

Ring in the New Year with these pretty pops. Make sure your resolutions include munching on these marshmallow treats!

Makes 12 Midnight Marshmallow Pops

1 (12-oz.) pkg. white candy coating Wafers

12 regular-size marshmallows

12 lollipop sticks or crystal lollipop sticks*

1 (1.5-oz.) can silver food coloring mist

silver dragées

12 white Necco Wafer candies

black edible marker

TIP

*Bling lollipop sticks were purchased at Hobby Lobby.

1. Melt the white candy coating Wafers according to the package instructions.
2. Push the lollipop sticks into one end of the marshmallows.
3. Holding the lollipop stick, dip the marshmallow into the melted candy coating.
4. Tap the stick on the side of the bowl to remove any excess. Place on parchment or wax paper to dry completely.
5. Lightly spray the marshmallows with silver food coloring mist.
6. Using a toothpick dipped in melted candy coating, draw a line around the bottom of the marshmallow and immediately attach the silver dragées.
7. Using a black edible marker, draw a simple clock face, making 4 dots spaced evenly around the edge of the white Necco Wafers and the hands of the clock at midnight.
8. Attach the Necco clock to the front of the marshmallow pop using the melted candy coating.

Pretty Party Hats

Glitzy party hats to top your favorite ice cream. Rolled in sparkling sugar and decorated with fun candy and sprinkles, these hats are a crafty treat that the kids will love to make!

Makes 12 Pretty Party Hats

12 sugar-style ice cream cones

1 (12-oz.) can frosting—vanilla for white and silver cones or chocolate for black cones

black, white, or silver sugar sprinkles

variety of sprinkles and candies like Sixlets, licorice lace, or sugar pearls

1. Carefully spread the frosting to fully cover the outside of the ice cream cone.
2. Pour a bottle of sugar sprinkles onto a shallow plate.
3. Roll the frosted cone into the sugar sprinkles to fully coat.
4. Using frosting, attach the sprinkles, Sixlet candies, or sugar pearls to decorate.

Norene Cox

Celebration Cupcakes

Your guests will bubble over when they see these adorable little cupcakes. Sparkle up some gummy cola bottles to top these cute little cuppies!

Makes 12 mini Celebration Cupcakes

12 mini cupcakes frosted white

½ cup white candy coating wafers

24 gummy cola bottle candies

green sugar sprinkles

12 yellow confetti sprinkles

white nonpareil sprinkles

clear sugar crystal sprinkles

TIP

To duplicate my champagne bucket look, place the mini cupcakes in a small paper nut cup sprayed with silver food coloring mist.

1. Sprinkle the top of the cupcake with the clear sugar crystals to resemble small ice cubes.

2. Melt the white candy coating wafers according to the package instructions.

3. Using a food safe paintbrush, brush the melted candy coating on the bottom ⅔ of the gummy cola bottle, leaving the neck of the bottle plain.

4. Immediately pour the green sugar sprinkles on the coated gummy bottle—make sure this is done over a small bowl to catch the excess sprinkles so they can be used again.

5. With a toothpick dipped in melted candy coating, attach a yellow confetti sprinkle on the front of the green gummy bottle. Place bottle on top of cupcake.

6. Cut a plain gummy cola bottle in half, turn it upside down, and dip the cut end into the melted candy coating.

7. Immediately dip it into a small bowl filled with white nonpareil sprinkles. This is the champagne glass. Place on top of the cupcake next to the green gummy champagne bottle.

Truffle Clocks

You can make this dessert in no time. An easy candy display for the countdown.

Makes 1 Truffle Clock

7 dark or milk chocolate truffles
6 white chocolate truffles
2 clear rock candy sticks

1. On a round platter, place 6 dark chocolate and 6 white chocolate truffles alternating in the place of clock numbers.
2. Push the ends of the clear rock candy sticks into a dark chocolate truffle so they rest at almost midnight. Place in the center of the platter.

Black Tie Party Penguins

Tuxedo treats for your black tie bash. Store-bought chocolate-covered graham cracker cookies dressed up all cute-like for the New Year.

Makes 12 Black Tie Party Penguins

½ cup white candy coating wafers

12 chocolate-covered graham cracker cookies

24 white confetti sprinkles

black edible marker

12 candy corn

1 chocolate bar

12 black confetti sprinkles

1. Melt the white candy coating wafers according to the package directions.
2. Dip the chocolate-covered graham cracker cookies halfway into the melted white candy coating.
3. Tip the bowl and cookie forward before lifting the cookie out so there is a little arch of the white coating on top for the tummy.
4. Draw a small dot in the middle of 2 white confetti sprinkles.
5. Using a toothpick dipped in white candy coating, attach the 2 white confetti sprinkles to the chocolate part near the top of the cookie for the eyes.
6. Slice the tip off a candy corn and attach it to the cookie with the melted candy coating under the eyes.
7. Cut 2 small triangles out of a chocolate bar. Attach to the top part of the white candy coating on the cookie with points facing each other for the bow tie.
8. Attach a small black confetti sprinkle in the center of the bow tie.

Sweet Champagne Flutes

Make a toast to the New Year with these sweet cakes! Festive flutes made of pound cake and cookies.

Makes 12 Sweet Champagne Flutes

½ cup white candy coating
  wafers

1 (10.75-oz.) pkg. frozen
  pound cake

12 vanilla sandwich cookies

white nonpareil sprinkles

white pearl sprinkles

1. Cut the pound cake into ½-inch slices (any thinner and the cake will break).
2. Next, trim off the pound cake slice into a long triangle. Cut off the tip of the triangle so it is flat.
3. Dip the top of the triangle into the melted candy coating. Immediately dip into the white nonpareil sprinkles. Place on parchment or wax paper to set.
4. With a toothpick dipped in the white candy coating, attach a few white pearl sprinkles to the front of the cake to resemble bubbles rising up the glass.
5. Dip the bottom of the triangle into the melted candy coating and place in the middle of the vanilla sandwich cookie. Hold until set.

Clock Cookies

Be the "tock" of the town when you make these timely treats. A perfect cookie favor to wrap up and take home as the party is winding down.

Makes 12 Clock Cookies

1 (7-oz.) pouch white cookie icing

12 Oreo cookies

48 silver dragées

black edible marker

1. Squeeze out a circle of icing around the top of an Oreo. Fill in the middle with icing.
2. Space 4 dragées evenly around the rim of the icing. Let dry completely.
3. With a black edible marker, make dots where the numbers should be. Draw on clock hands set at midnight.

Norene Cox

ACKNOWLEDGMENTS

To all of the wonderful, sweet folks who take the time to check out what's happening on my website, www.partypinching.com, and who follow *Party Pinching* on Facebook, Twitter, Pinterest, and Instagram, thank you for your love and support. Your comments and emails really do mean the world to me. Please know that I sincerely appreciate each and every one of you for coming along with me on this candy-coated journey!

Thank you to my two super sweet boys, Austin and Carson. Every little milestone on this amazing adventure, you were both there to say, "Good job, Mom. " You have no idea how much your encouraging words mean to me. I am thankful that you were both so excited to have me be your room mom when you were little, so thankful for the young men you are becoming, and for always making me laugh. You both give me a reason to celebrate each and every day and I love you both more than you can ever know. I am beyond blessed to have the honor of being your mom.

Travis, my cupcake lovin' man, you have been my biggest fan from day one. You are the one who encouraged me to start my blog and share my cute food and party ideas. Thank you for telling me how proud you are of me and for your amazing support, understanding and encouragement. Thanks mostly for the surprise trip to Vegas just when I needed it—you are the best husband in the world and the love of my life. I am one lucky lady.

Thank you to my cute mom, who instilled in me the need to feed every person who walks through my door, for encouraging me to be creative, and for being so excited for me every step of the way. To my adorable dad, the person I inherited my sweet tooth from, thank you for being so proud of me. It was sweet how you bragged about me to everyone, and I miss you every day. I will always love you both with all of my heart.

To my sisters, Evelyn and Merry and their families, who I love so much, thank you for cheering me on and sharing my treat ideas with all of your friends and coworkers.

A heartfelt thank you to Joanna Barker, Hannah Ballard, Bekah Claussen, Rodney Fife, Rozelle Hansen, Rachel Munk, and the entire Cedar Fort Publishing team. You turned a life-long dream of mine into a reality with your expertise and confidence in my work. Thank you for believing in me, for your guidance, for your encouraging words, and for all of your hard work. I am forever grateful.

Thank you to Mindy Cone of *Creative Juice*. You believed in me and this is the result. You are as sweet as your beautiful *Gourmet French Macarons* book.

A sincere thank you to Kate Huisentruit, Margaret Larson, Steve Wilson, Suzie Wiley, and the entire *New Day Northwest* team. You're such a genuine group of people and it's a privilege for me to be a guest on your show.

Thank you to Cindi Benoit, Maria Fox, Kit Schorzman, and the entire staff at Wight's Home & Garden. It is truly an honor to have you as my sponsor. You folks are a wonderland of sweetness.

I have been fortunate to be surrounded by amazing ladies that have been my support from day one. They have listened, advised, and contributed above and beyond in so many ways to the success of my blog and my book. Thank you to Mindy Cone, Christie Colla, Melissa Diamond, Do Driver, Barb Eli, Tiffany Fox, Cathy Gellis, Janine Hauser, Tina Jordan, Jillian Tohber Leslie, Kristy McCarthy, Lydia Menzies, Monica Meuse, Jill Mills, Patti Mroczek, and Victoria Threader. Thank you for lifting me up and for always being there for me.

Thanks to my incredible, wonderful friends and family who have nicknamed me Martha. I love you all. Your encouraging words, comments on Facebook, phone calls, texts, letters, and hugs have filled me up and kept me going. I am truly blessed.

To the entire party, cakey, and food blogging communities, thank you for welcoming me in, showing me the ropes, and supporting me both personally and professionally. I am constantly amazed, inspired, and in awe of the talent in these groups. You have shared, encouraged, laughed, and cried along with me. You have taught me words like adorbs, totes, and other sayings to annoy my teen boys. You are the best friends I have never met. The outpouring of support and love that you have shown me is overwhelming and I admire you all. For realz.

Thank you to Picnic Point Elementary. Where it all started.

Finally, thank you to my beagle, Kurby, for controlling your hound instincts (most of the time) when I was photographing food, and for lying across my laptop when you felt I was working too much. I didn't rescue you; it was the other way around.

131

About the Author

When Norene's sons became teenagers, she realized how much she missed being a room mom. Making sweet treats with the kids and throwing classroom parties were all a thing of the past. As a result, she created *Party Pinching*, a popular website where she could blog about her cute food and budget-friendly party ideas. Her adorable desserts have been praised by *Family Fun* magazine, *Seventeen* magazine, *Taste of Home*, and even Martha Stewart herself! She is a frequent guest on *New Day Northwest*, a morning television show in Seattle where her easy dessert demonstrations get rave reviews. Norene lives in the Seattle area with her husband, two sons, and a beagle. Visit Norene's website, *Party Pinching*, at www.partypinching.com.

Cooking Measurement Equivalents

Cups	Tablespoons	Fluid Ounces
⅛ cup	2 Tbsp.	1 fl. oz.
¼ cup	4 Tbsp.	2 fl. oz.
⅓ cup	5 Tbsp. + 1 tsp.	
½ cup	8 Tbsp.	4 fl. oz.
⅔ cup	10 Tbsp. + 2 tsp.	
¾ cup	12 Tbsp.	6 fl. oz.
1 cup	16 Tbsp.	8 fl. oz.

Cups	Fluid Ounces	Pints/Quarts/Gallons
1 cup	8 fl. oz.	½ pint
2 cups	16 fl. oz.	1 pint = ½ quart
3 cups	24 fl. oz.	1½ pints
4 cups	32 fl. oz.	2 pints = 1 quart
8 cups	64 fl. oz.	2 quarts = ½ gallon
16 cups	128 fl. oz.	4 quarts = 1 gallon

Other Helpful Equivalents

1 Tbsp.	3 tsp.
8 oz.	½ lb.
16 oz.	1 lb.

Metric Measurement Equivalents

Approximate Weight Equivalents

Ounces	Pounds	Grams
4 oz.	¼ lb.	113 g
5 oz.		142 g
6 oz.		170 g
8 oz.	½ lb.	227 g
9 oz.		255 g
12 oz.	¾ lb.	340 g
16 oz.	1 lb.	454 g

Approximate Volume Equivalents

Cups	US Fluid Ounces	Milliliters
⅛ cup	1 fl. oz.	30 ml
¼ cup	2 fl. oz.	59 ml
½ cup	4 fl. oz.	118 ml
¾ cup	6 fl. oz.	177 ml
1 cup	8 fl. oz.	237 ml

Other Helpful Equivalents

½ tsp.	2½ ml
1 tsp.	5 ml
1 Tbsp.	15 ml

Index

Index